THE LITTLE FLOWER OF JESUS

STORY BY
SISTER M. JULITA, S.S.N.D.

PICTURES BY
SISTER M. JOHN VIANNEY, S.S.N.D.

Neumann Press
Charlotte, North Carolina

THE LITTLE FLOWER OF JESUS

1960 Ecclesiastical Permission

A Little Flower of Jesus

ISBN: 978-1-930873-98-8

Printed and bound in India.

Neumann Press
Charlotte, North Carolina
www.NeumannPress.com

2013

IT WAS NIGHT. One by one the lights of the houses were going out. Even the streetcars stood still in their barns. Only the feathery snowflakes danced gaily about hour after hour. Like little stars they clung to the bare branches of the trees. They covered the roofs of houses. They covered the doorsteps and gardens. They covered the streets and sidewalks, even the tops of fences. They settled on tall telephone poles and the long, thin black wires. The city slept under the white blanket of the fresh soft snow.

But in one pretty house of red brick and white stone, light was peeking through the windows. In this house four little girls were huddled together in the large living room listening to the crackling of the fresh logs in the fireplace and the ticking of the big clock in the hall.

It was late but the girls were not at all sleepy or tired. Their eyes were still very bright. Their hearts were very happy. It was ten days after Christmas, and they were still excited. When they were opening their gifts from the Christ Child, Mother and Daddy told them that soon there would be another surprise. The Christ Child would come again, but not with

red and white candy canes, or pretty dolls and fluffy dogs. This time He would bring a brand new baby. This was the night of the big surprise and, of course, they were not sleepy.

The big clock in the hall struck loud and strong. Leonie and Celine, the two youngest, counted, “One, two, three, four, five, six, seven, eight, nine, ten, eleven, twelve!”

“It’s midnight!” said Marie. And the three girls smiled as they looked at their big sister.

It was fun staying up until midnight. It was fun waiting for the surprise. The two older girls continued to turn the pages of their scrapbook while the younger ones put their paper dolls to sleep.

Then all of a sudden the door opened. There stood Father with a big smile on his face.

"You have a new baby sister," he said. At once he gathered Celine, the tiniest little girl, in his big strong arms and went up the stairs. Hand in hand the others followed. In a very short time they all stood at the foot of the new baby's cradle. No night could have been lovelier or brighter or whiter than this! It seemed that the thousands of the starry snowflakes came down to earth to welcome their new little sister.

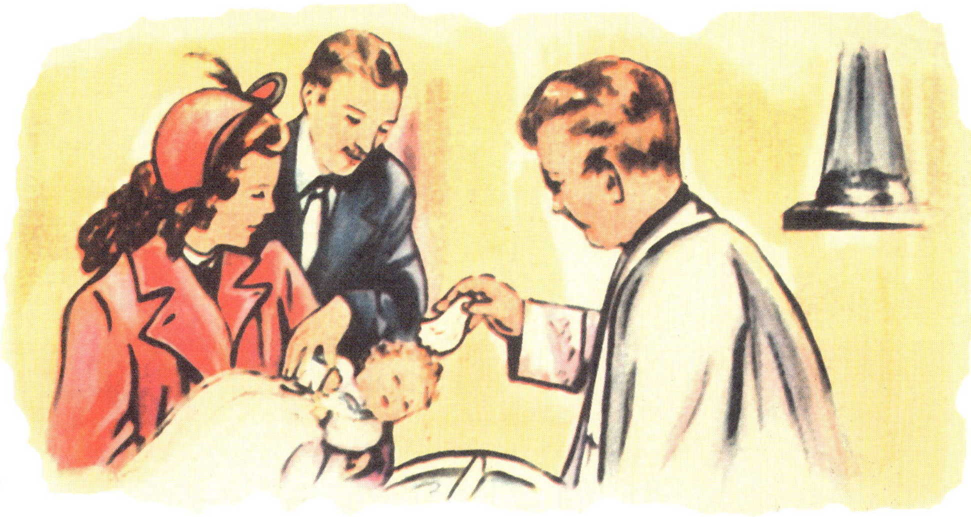

Two days later while the snow was still very white and deep, there was much joy in the pretty house on the quiet street. This was the day when the new baby was taken to the big church to become a child of God.

Marie was the godmother. How carefully she held the little bundle in her arms. The baby was no bigger than her favorite doll. The other girls saw the priest pour holy water on the head of the new baby. They heard his strong voice saying, "Marie Frances Therese, I baptize you in the name of the Father, and of the Son, and of the Holy Ghost."

Mother, Daddy, and the four sisters thought they were as happy as the angels in heaven because at this moment the baby's soul became the home of God the Father, the Son, and the Holy Ghost.

It was fun taking care of this tiny little sister. The girls took turns humming her to sleep. They watched her smile to the angels in her dreams. They were all around her little crib as soon as she opened her pretty eyes after her long naps. Then one day Mother looked very worried. Everyone was sad. Little Therese was very sick. The whole family stood very quietly around the little cradle. The baby looked as if she was not alive.

"Will this baby die just like my four other little babies?" Mother cried. "Dear God, help us!" she prayed with her whole

heart. "Dear Saint Joseph, you loved Jesus so much. You took such good care of Him when He was a baby. You took care of Mary, His Blessed Mother. Please help me. Please make my baby well!"

Hardly had she finished her prayer when all of a sudden the baby seemed to live. She opened her pretty blue eyes and smiled for Mother. From that moment she began to grow stronger. Her cheeks became pink. The smile that she gave everyone was as bright as a sunbeam. Everyone in the stone house was happy again.

Soon Therese learned how to walk and talk. Everyone loved her and she loved everyone. Whenever Mr. Martin would come home from his shop where he fixed watches and clocks Little Therese would run to meet him. "A ride, Daddy, a ride!" she would say. And Mr. Martin would play the favorite game of ride-a-cock-horse with her. Little Therese would sit on one of his boots and go for a long ride. Then he would take her in his arms, lift her high in the air, and carry her on his shoulders.

"Aren't you spoiling her?" Mother asked.

But Mr. Martin looked at his smiling little girl, patted her curly golden head, and said with a twinkle in his eye, "Well, why not? She is my Little Queen!"

Mother, Daddy, and the five girls spent many happy days together. They prayed together, worked together, and played together. By her merry chatter and cheery laughs Little Therese brought much joy and sunshine to her home.

When Mrs. Martin sat at the large window in the living room, making beautiful lace, Little Therese would not leave her for a moment. She played with her bird cage, her dolls, and other toys. One day she learned something new. She could walk stairs all by herself. Placing her little feet on a step which was almost too high for her, Therese would turn toward her mother and call, "Mother! Mother!" Mrs. Martin would then look up from her work and answer, "Yes, darling!" If she did not, Therese would become sad and just stand still and never move.

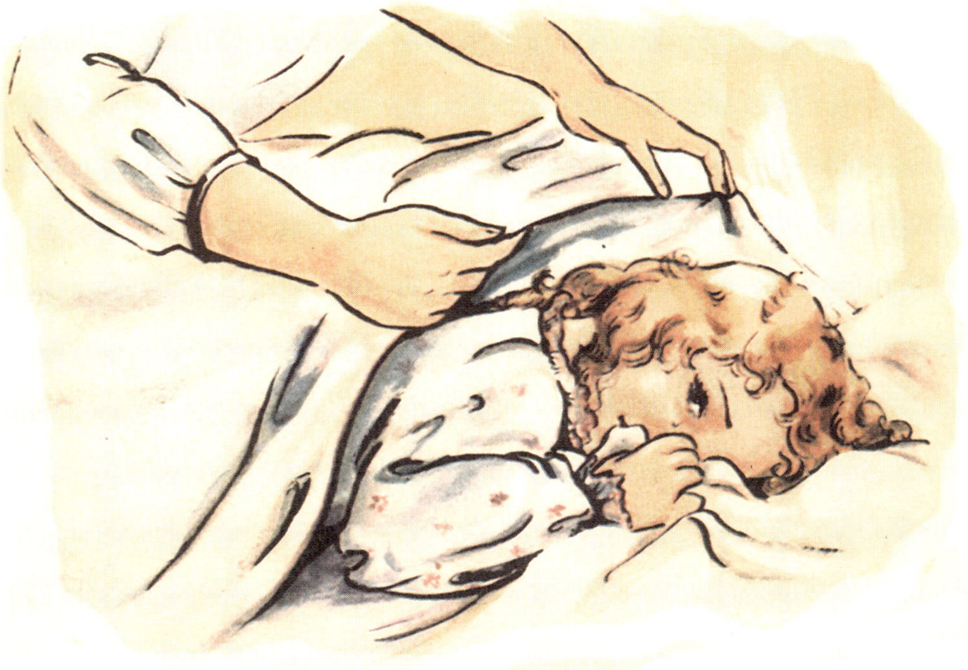

Therese had faults like other little girls. Sometimes Mother and Daddy or one of her sisters would have to tell her that there was a better way of doing things. Then Therese would be sorry and promise to try. And she kept her promise.

One morning Mother wanted to kiss Therese before going to church. When she came to her bed Therese was hidden under the blankets. Just like a spoiled child, she said, "I don't want anyone to look at me."

When Mother heard Therese talk like this she left the room. Two minutes later Therese ran to her. "Mother! Mother!" she cried hugging her. "I was naughty. Please forgive me."

One day, without saying a word to anyone, Therese climbed the stairs. Up, up she went until she reached the second floor. How happy she was! She smiled as she looked down the flight of stairs. Then she turned and walked to Marie's doorway. The door was locked. She reached for the knob but was too small to even touch it. She stood on her tiptoes but the knob was still too high. She pushed the door but it would not open. Once again she tried to reach. She did not call for anyone to help. She did not begin to cry. Little Therese just put herself flat on the floor and would not move. Her big sister, Marie, saw what was going on. She was ready to run and help her, but Mother said, "Marie, you must let Therese do that herself or ask for help."

Marie whispered to Therese, "Darling, you are not pleasing to the Infant Jesus when you act so stubborn."

Not pleasing to the Infant Jesus! Little Therese loved the Infant Jesus too much to displease Him. She was sorry and said, "I will never, never do that again." From that day on Little Therese tried to please Jesus. To say "Yes" to Jesus meant that Therese would have to be willing to do all Mother and Daddy and her sisters asked her to do. It meant never to be stubborn or selfish. After this only her Guardian Angel would know of all the little secrets she planned to make Jesus happy.

"She says her prayers like an angel and knows how to talk to God," her mother wrote to an aunt. Yes, Therese thought much of God, of heaven, and of the saints. Even when she was a small girl she said that she would never be afraid of God. The garden, trees, flowers, and sky told her but one thing, that God loved her. Her little heart seemed much too small to hold all the love that she wanted to give to God.

When Therese was five years old, Mrs. Martin became very sick. No medicine could help her. Day after day she grew worse. Day after day the whole family prayed. God wanted Mrs. Martin in heaven. One night Father called the girls. They all gathered for the last time at Mother's bed. She could only look at them. She looked at Marie, Pauline, Leonie, Celine, and her Little Therese. In a few minutes all was over and her soul went to heaven.

Father lifted Therese up gently and said, "Come and kiss your mother for the last time." And Therese kissed her mother without a word.

It was a sad day in the stone house. Father and the five girls came home after the funeral. The house seemed so different without Mother. How they missed her. Leonie with big tears in her eyes ran to the oldest sister, "Marie, Marie, please be my mother now."

And Therese thought, "Pauline will be sad if she hasn't any little girl to love." In a minute she was standing at Pauline's

side. "Pauline, will you be my mother now?" she asked. And so Pauline became Therese's little mother. She taught her many ways of doing little things for God.

"Have I been good today? Is Jesus pleased with me?" Therese asked her little mother each evening as she tucked her into bed. Only when she was sure that she pleased Jesus was Therese happy. Then only would she fall asleep.

One day Pauline and Therese planned a surprise for Father. When he came home from work Therese met him at the door. "Daddy, Daddy," she cried, "I know how to read." So on his knee she hopped with the book wide open. And the first word Therese read was "Heaven." Even now she was thinking of God's beautiful heaven, the angels, and the saints.

Every day, Therese and Celine and her cousin, Marie, walked to school together. On the way they laughed and talked. In class there was much to learn. Therese loved books. She liked to study and read. But when the bell rang for recess many times Therese was sad. She was not good at playing noisy games. There were some little girls from her class who were jealous of her. At recess time they would make fun of her, tease her, and even call her names. Many times Therese would have a hard time trying to hide her tears. Best of all she liked to sit under a shady tree in the schoolyard and tell stories to some of her friends. The girls said that no one could tell stories as well as Therese.

At four o'clock in the afternoon Therese was always happy. It was then that the girls started on their way home. She would then forget all her sorrows and troubles because she liked nothing better than the happy evenings with her father. Just as Therese was his "little queen," he was her "king." On holidays and free days they spent many hours together, fishing and hiking.

One evening Father and his "little queen" were out walking. It was a beautiful quiet night. The sky was dark and hundreds of stars twinkled merrily. "Lead me, Daddy," she called. She took her father's hand and walked along, looking only at the beautiful starry sky. "How great and good God must be!" she said.

Then all at once Therese stopped and cried, "Oh, Daddy, look! My name is written in heaven." And she pointed to the stars. "There it is!" Father looked up and saw a cluster of twinkling stars forming the letter T.

One day God was asking Therese for another sacrifice. This time Pauline, "her little mother," was leaving home. She offered her life to Jesus and would become a Sister. Therese loved her "little mother" very much. Just how much she missed her no one ever knew. This was a secret between her and Jesus.

Then one day during the Easter holidays, when Mr. Martin and the girls were getting ready to go to the country for a vacation, Therese became sick. Her head began to ache. She was weak and tired. The big sisters put her to bed, hoping that by morning Therese would feel better. But when morning came Therese was worse. Poor Mr. Martin! In the evening several doctors were called to help the little girl. But they only shook their heads. After long talks with each other they could not help her. She was getting weaker with every minute. No medicine or pills seemed to make her well.

In Therese's room there was a beautiful statue of our Lady, a statue which Therese loved very much. The girls knelt down before this statue. "Oh, dear Mother of God," they begged with tears in their eyes, "make our little sister well!"

Therese also prayed, and something wonderful happened. It seemed as if the statue became alive. Our Blessed Lady became very beautiful with a heavenly smile on her face. She came to Therese and stood by her bed and Therese became well.

“Our Lady is so beautiful!” Therese said over and over again. And then she looked at the statue and said, “I am more lucky than you are, dear Mary, because I have you for a mother to love. If I were the Queen of heaven and you Therese, I would wish to be Therese that I might see you, the Queen of heaven!”

On a beautiful day in May when the birds were chirping their May songs and the lilacs and tulips were blooming, and the grass was fresh and green, Therese woke up very early. This was the day of her First Communion. Her pretty white lace dress and veil were all ready for her. Most of all, her little heart could hardly wait until Jesus would come. "I love You, dear Jesus! I give myself to You forever! was all that she could say when Jesus came to her heart.

"Why is she crying?" some ladies whispered in church. "Does Therese miss her mother? Does she miss Pauline?"

No one but Jesus knew of Therese's secret. She was so happy

to have heaven in her heart. She was a little flower that God loved very much. That afternoon Therese and her father visited her "little mother" in the Carmelite convent. Mr. Martin had given her a beautiful present. It was a little golden watch. Therese had many joys that day but the greatest joy was the visit of her God.

Then came another good-by. This time, Marie, her other big sister, was leaving for the convent. By this time Therese knew that some day she, too, would offer herself to Jesus. She wanted to give Him everything.

One day Therese told her "king" about her secret. She told him how much she wanted to be God's little flower. She too wanted to become a Sister. When Therese asked the Sisters to take her, they only shook their heads and said, "No!" She was much too young. She did not give up. Maybe the Bishop will say "Yes." But he looked at her and said, "No!" He, too, said, "You are too young."

Therese did not give up. She traveled to Rome with her father to see the Holy Father. Surely he could not refuse her. The Holy Father looked at the young girl. He shook his head and smiled. Then he said, "No, you are too young!"

Therese came home sad. She was disappointed, but she did not give up. She prayed. After several months, just before her fifteenth birthday the answer came. This time the Sisters said, "Yes!" Therese was happy.

This was a joy and yet it meant another sacrifice. She said good-by to her dear "king" whom she loved very much. She left her beautiful home and came to the Carmelite convent. It is there that she became a great saint. She was called Sister Therese of the Child Jesus. She never did big things as many saints have done. Whatever she did was done with much love, even picking up a tiny pin from the floor. She never complained about the cold. No work was too hard for her. She was never too busy to help the other Sisters. She was always pleasant and happy and even smiled when she had to do things that were not easy.

Nine years passed very quickly. One spring Sister Therese began to cough. She was very tired. Soon she became so weak that she could not work any more. She could not go to the chapel to pray with the other Sisters, but spent most of her time in bed, suffering and praying. The Sisters could see that soon she would leave them. Sister Therese was going to die. The doctor could not help her.

"Don't be sad," she said to the Sisters. "I will spend my heaven doing good on earth. I will send down a shower of roses!" She told them that she would not rest until the end of the world. She would work for Jesus even in heaven.

Then on a beautiful day in late summer when the days were becoming shorter, when the late summer flowers were still in bloom, and when the birds were beginning to leave for their homes in the south, Sister Therese was dying. It was evening. The church bells began to ring at six o'clock to remind everyone to say the Hail Mary.

Sister Therese heard the bells. She was beginning her last hour on earth. The Sisters gathered around her bed. She could not speak to them but she looked at each one and smiled.

Then suddenly, although very weak, she sat up in bed and raised her arms. "My God, I love Thee!" she cried. In her eyes there was a heavenly light. Then her eyes closed and her beautiful soul went to God.

Hardly anyone heard of Sister Therese of the Child Jesus when she lived on earth. Only her family and the Sisters knew her. Soon after her death everyone began to talk about Sister Therese. Even now, in every part of the world, people are praying to her and asking her for favors. You can see her statue or her picture in many churches and homes. She is holding a bouquet of beautiful roses. But beneath the roses Saint Therese is holding something else. She is holding a cross. A cross? Yes. This is to tell us that the Little Flower of Jesus did everything, even suffered, out of love for Jesus.